THE BUILDING OF STONEHENGE

⚠ **WARNING:**
CHOKING HAZARD–Small parts.
Not for children under 3 years.

THE BUILDING OF STONEHENGE

Written by
MORGAN BEARD

Illustrated by
AMY GRIMES

RP MINIS

PHILADELPHIA

RP Minis®
Hachette Book Group
1290 Avenue of the Americas, New York, NY 10104
www.runningpress.com
@Running_Press

Originally published October 2006, second revised edition October 2025.

Published by RP Minis, an imprint of Hachette Book Group, Inc. The RP Minis name and logo is a registered trademark of Hachette Book Group, Inc.

Contact specialmarkets@hbgusa.com regarding special discounts for bulk purchases.

The publisher is not responsible for websites (or their content) that are not owned by the publisher.

Design by Susan Van Horn

ISBN: 979-8-89414-177-0

Made in Dongguan, China (HKD) 06/25 #01

CONTENTS

INTRODUCTION

Everyone loves a mystery, and few mysteries have captured people's imaginations like the ruins of Stonehenge. This ancient stone arrangement rests in the Salisbury Plain in Wiltshire, Southern England, and contains over 150 rocks, some weighing forty metric tons (or the equivalent weight of six elephants). Stonehenge has fascinated visitors for over five millennia, and yet, the who, how, and why remain pure

speculation. Modern science has begun to shed light on these mysteries by using new technology like radio-carbon dating and computers, but most of Stonehenge's secrets are as elusive and intriguing as ever.

THE BUILDERS

Over the years, a variety of people, cultures, and species have been given credit for the building of Stonehenge. Some of the most legendary figures thought to be responsible for this monument have included:

Giants: According to old myths, dancing giants were caught in a sunbeam and petrified to stone, causing the monument to be nicknamed the "Giant's Ring."

Merlin and King Arthur: Some believe Merlin himself assembled Stonehenge to commemorate slain chieftains. It's also rumored the Sword in the Stone, which would eventually lead Arthur onto the throne and into legend, was made from a Stonehenge stone.

Aliens: Most of the world's earliest and elaborate crop circles are found within a forty-mile (64 km) radius of Stonehenge. Scientists today are still unable to replicate these crop circles, suggesting their construction and that of Stonehenge should perhaps be credited to a more intelligent species.

Atlanteans: According to Plato, the Kingdom of Atlantis controlled the islands of the Atlantic and built many stone structures to better predict future events based on astronomical calculations.

Druids: John Aubrey, a Stonehenge scholar, erroneously suggested this connection three centuries ago. The Druids are an earth-based faith we now know formed much later than the building of Stonehenge.

It is almost easier to believe magic created Stonehenge than to acknowledge that, mind-bogglingly enough, it was probably done by societies yet to invent the wheel. Current archaeological evidence suggests three societies built the monument over a two-thousand-year period. There is still contention about which people are responsible and for what, but the general consensus is ancient Britons built the site.

The **Beaker Folk** from 2500 BC are believed to have done work on

Stonehenge. They were an aggressive culture who invaded the Salisbury Plain. From artifacts, we know the Beakers were sophisticated, organized, understood mathematics, worshipped the sun, and celebrated the solstices. This makes them ideal builders for some of the site.

The other cultures who contributed to Stonehenge remain a mystery, though archaeologists are getting closer and closer to finding answers.

CREATING STONEHENGE

Appropriately enough, Stonehenge started in the Stone Age. Up to three prehistoric cultures poured a combined thirty million hours of labor into the three-phase project, and the result is a stunning reminder of the creativity, intelligence, and technology possessed by our ancient ancestors.

PHASE I

Almost five thousand years ago in about 3100 BC, the first construction began. A circular ditch nearly 288 feet (87 m) in diameter was dug, and 56 wooden posts were placed within it. These wooden posts were inserted into **Aubrey Holes**, named after their discoverer, John Aubrey. Four **Station Stones** were also probably placed perpendicular to the midsummer sunrise during this phase, but there is debate suggesting this might have happened later on.

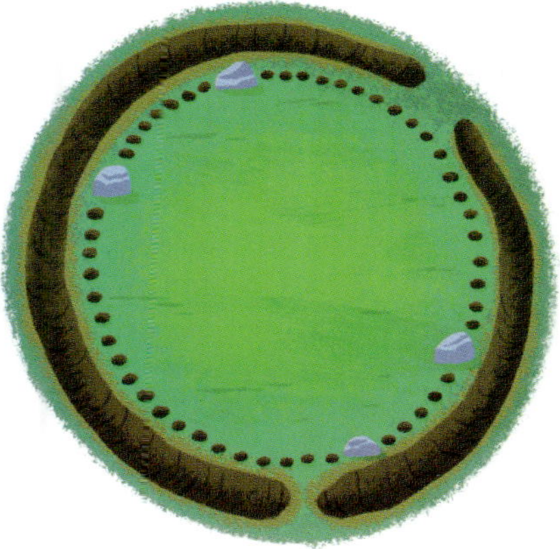

PHASE II

The Beaker Folk are believed to have contributed to this phase. They moved a number of **bluestones**, each weighing about four metric tons, 240 miles (386 km) from rock quarries in the Preseli Mountains. These stones were transported over rivers and open seas and moved on land by pushing sledges over a series of rolling logs.

The Beakers set the bluestones in an incomplete double circle, enlarged the ditch and added the **"Avenue"** to the site. The Avenue would eventually

run nearly two miles from the River Avon to the northeastern entrance of Stonehenge with parallel banks. This pathway was probably a ceremonial entrance, as it is aligned with the midsummer sunrise. The Beakers also placed the **Heel Stone**, weighing thirty-two metric tons, in the Avenue.

The Beaker's vision for Stonehenge was ambitious but never completed. The site was abandoned around 2500 BC.

This phase is also a bit contested. Some believe the bluestones weren't moved until Phase III and Phase II saw only the building of a timber circle.

PHASE III

Around 2300 BC, Stonehenge was built into what we see today. To create this finished appearance, sarsen rock, a type of sandstone, was transported twenty miles (32 km) from Marlborough Downs using sledges and log-rollers. The rock was then fashioned with "mauls," a type of hammer, to shape the surfaces.

Thirty of these neatly trimmed stones went into the **Sarsen Circle**. Each of the thirty was about thirteen feet high (4 m), over six feet wide (2 m), and three feet thick (1 m). They were capped with lintels, or horizontal stones, hoisted with a complicated leverage system on top of these base stones. Hammered to curve in a circle and with joints to secure the stones, these lintels created a thirteen-foot-high (4 m) circle in the air—a height kept consistent all the way around to within a few

centimeters. This precise calculation and tooling makes the Sarsen Circle the most impressive feature of Stonehenge.

The largest features of Stonehenge are the **Trilithons**, which are the largest sarsen stones forming the horseshoe shape in the center of the Sarsen Circle. These stones weigh up to forty metric tons with the largest, the **Grand Trilithon**, up to twenty-seven feet (8 m) tall. They were erected in five pairs with five lintels to top the formation.

The **Altar Stone** and **Slaughter Stone** were also added to the structure. Despite their names, the stones were never used as an altar or for slaughter. The Altar Stone lies directly in front of the Grand Trilithon and is the only rock made of green sandstone. The sarsen Slaughter Stone is near the northeast entrance of Stonehenge. The bluestones were also reused, set in a single ring within the Sarsen Circle and in an inner horseshoe inside the Trilithon formation.

The last modifications to Stonehenge took place between 1900 BC and 1700 BC. A series of holes, dubbed the **Y and Z holes**, were dug in concentric circles between the Sarsen Circle and the Aubrey Holes. These holes were meant to hold even more stones, but construction was halted, leaving the site abandoned once more.

THE PRESENT DAY

Stonehenge has had its share of visitors over the years, and not all of them meant well. Locals and conquerors alike dismantled and destroyed parts of the site. It wasn't until very recently, AD 1918, the site was transferred from private property to the British government, finally acknowledging its historical value. In AD 1986, it was honored as a World Heritage Site and has received a wealth of support since then.

WRITTEN IN STONE

We have some information about how the stones were placed and by whom, but when it comes to why, there is very little to go on.

The most plausible explanation is Stonehenge was used as a calendar or an ancient observatory. There are several alignments between the stones and the sun and the moon, including the midsummer sunrise over the Heel Stone and a midwinter sunset in between the uprights of the Grand Trilithon.

The mathematics of these alignments required the builders of Stonehenge to apply principles of Pythagorean Theorem and pi ages before these concepts were fully discovered by the rest of the Western world. This demonstration of genius makes the possibilities for Stonehenge's true purpose nearly infinite.

While Stonehenge could easily have been an ancient observatory for the stars, there's no reason it couldn't have been a temple as well; it was often the priests' job to keep track of the stars' movements.

Of course, these potential uses for Stonehenge don't answer the question of why a temple or observatory would need to be built in the middle of Salisbury Plain, such a long distance from rock quarries. One theory which does answer this question is that of ley lines. Some suggest the world is covered in high-energy force fields, called ley lines, and intersections of these lines are high-power areas.

Stonehenge is believed to lie on one of these intersections.

Whatever its purpose, it's clear the site was important to these prehistoric people, and because of the many wonders and possibilities it continues to offer us today, Stonehenge maintains its importance in the modern world.

BUILD YOUR OWN

First, take out the pieces for the puzzle map and put them together (if pieces have trouble staying together flip the pieces over, assemble the puzzle upside down using back text as a guide, and tape pieces together). Next, look at the numbers on the mat corresponding to the numbers on the bottom of your stone pieces. Place your stone pieces on the matching numbers on the mat. Arrange stones 11 and 12 with their lintels resting on